Thud!

by Cara Torrance

illustrated by Becky Down

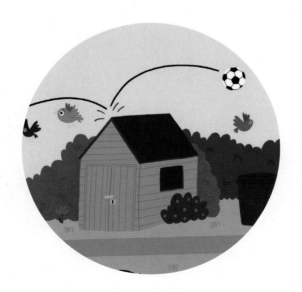

OXFORD
UNIVERSITY PRESS
AUSTRALIA & NEW ZEALAND

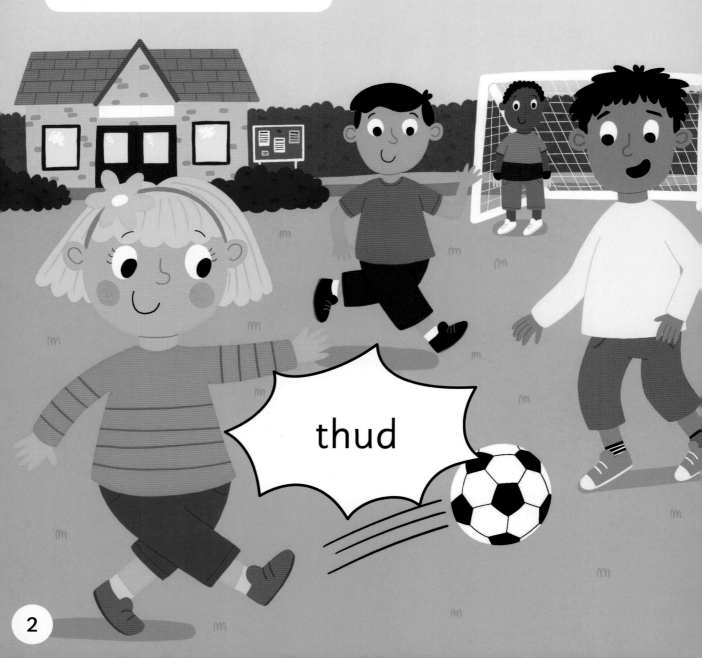

Zak kicks.

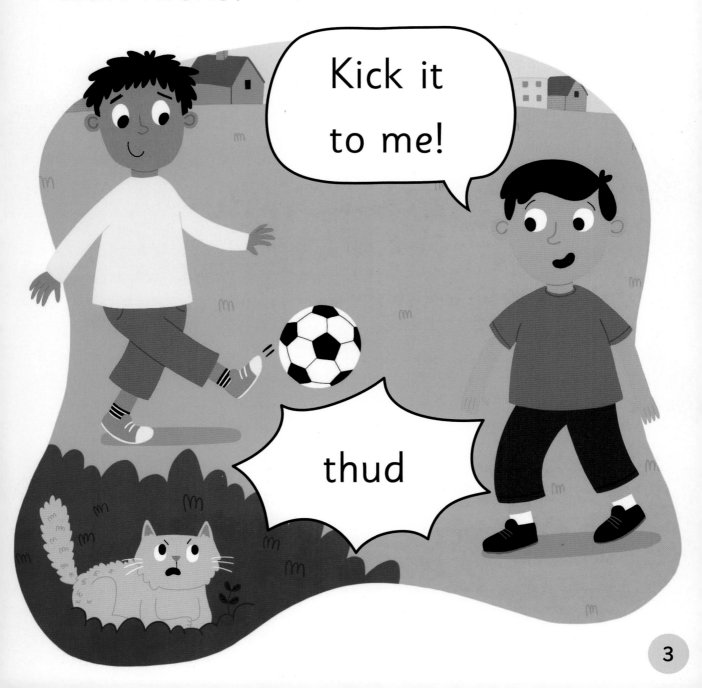

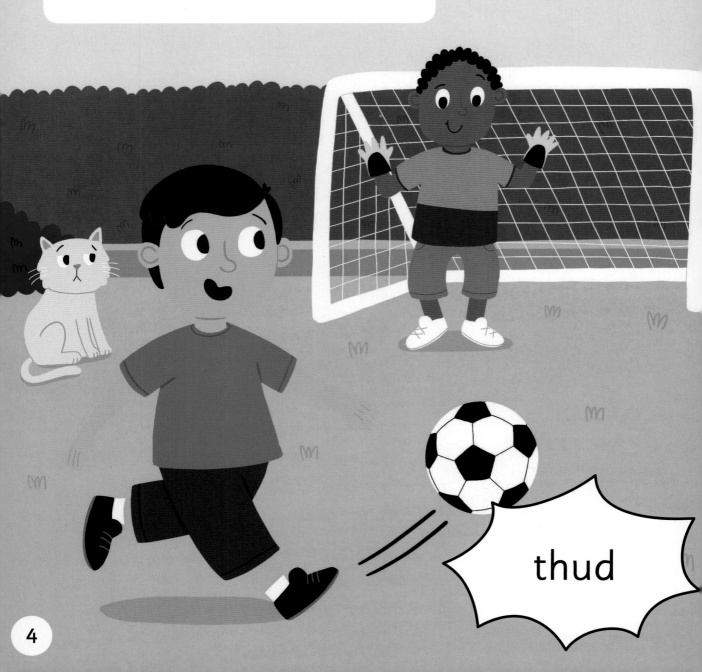

Bill runs.

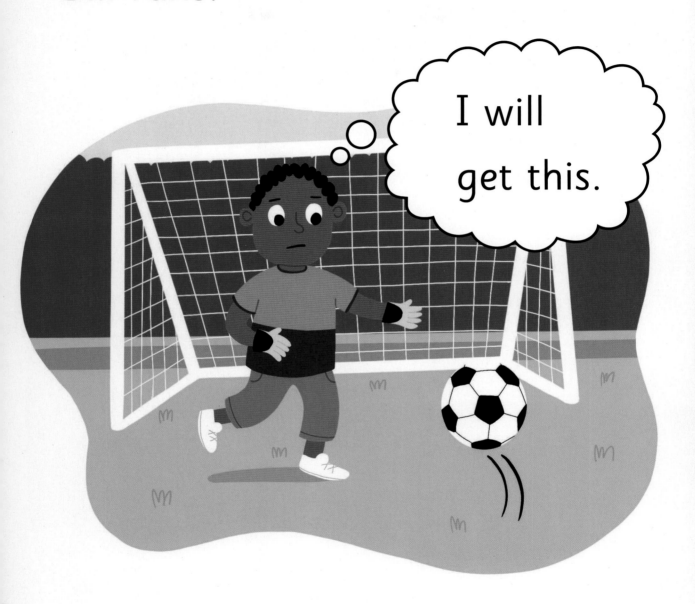

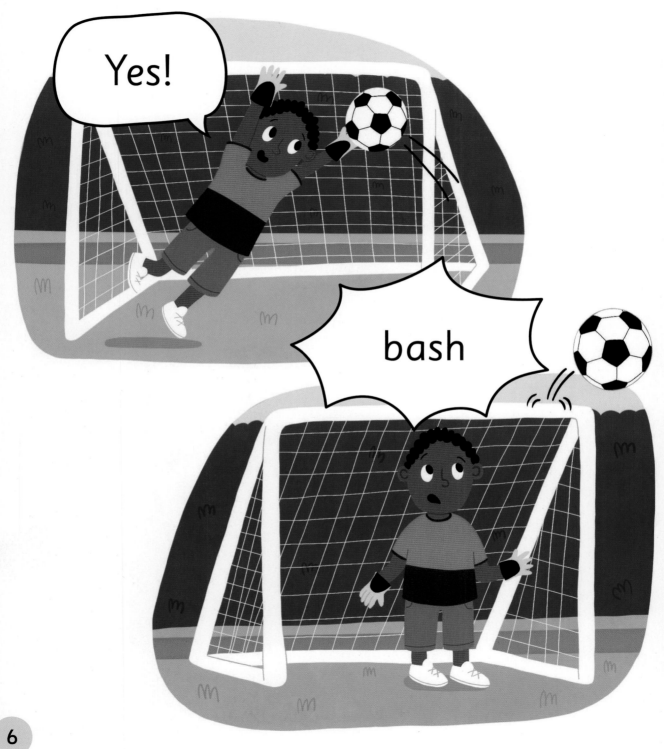

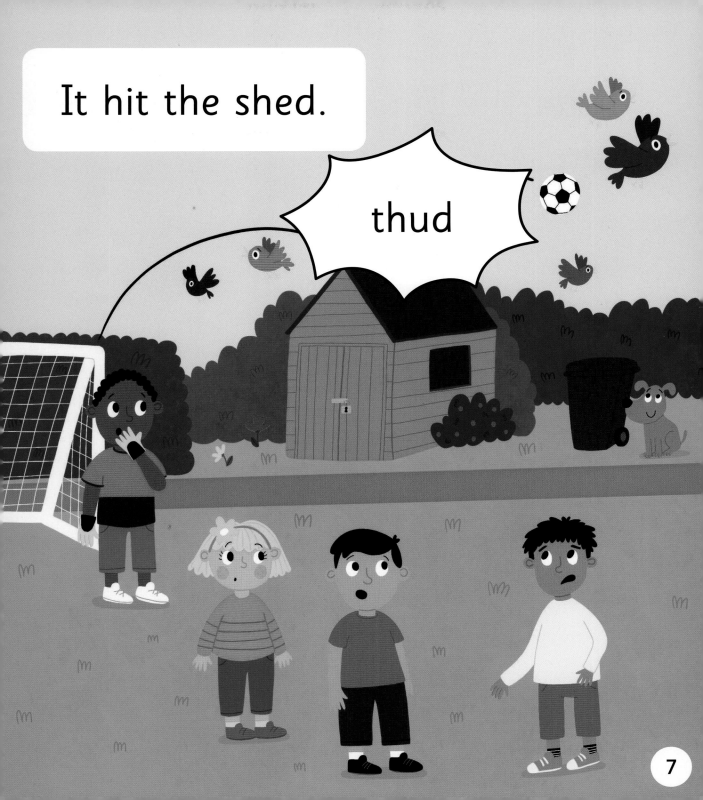

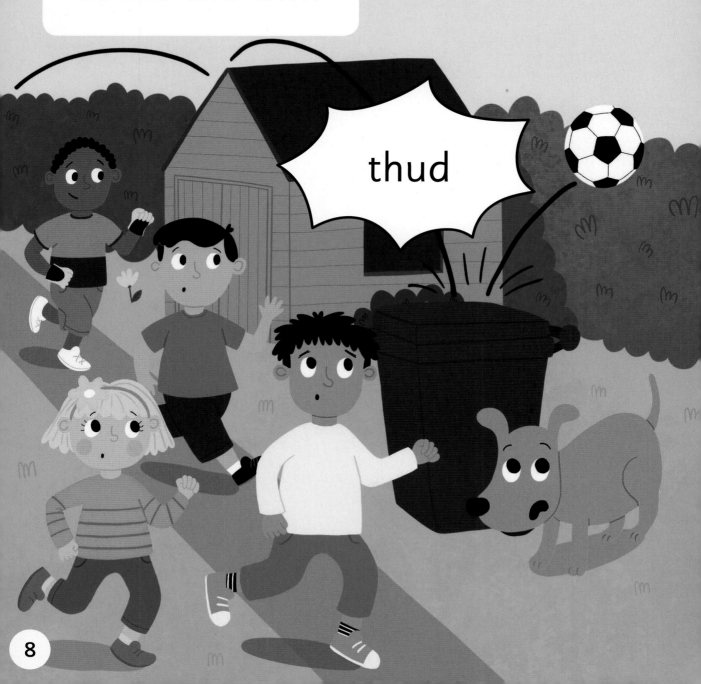

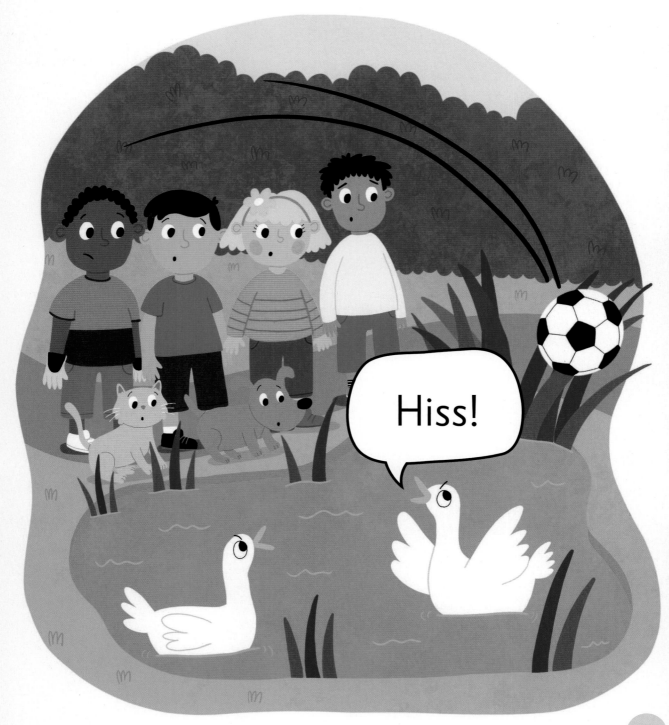

Anna, Zak, Hung and Bill run.

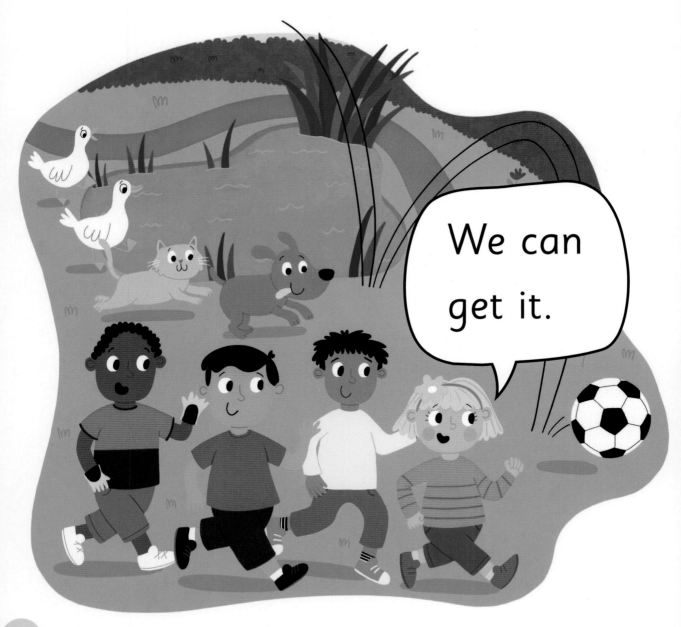

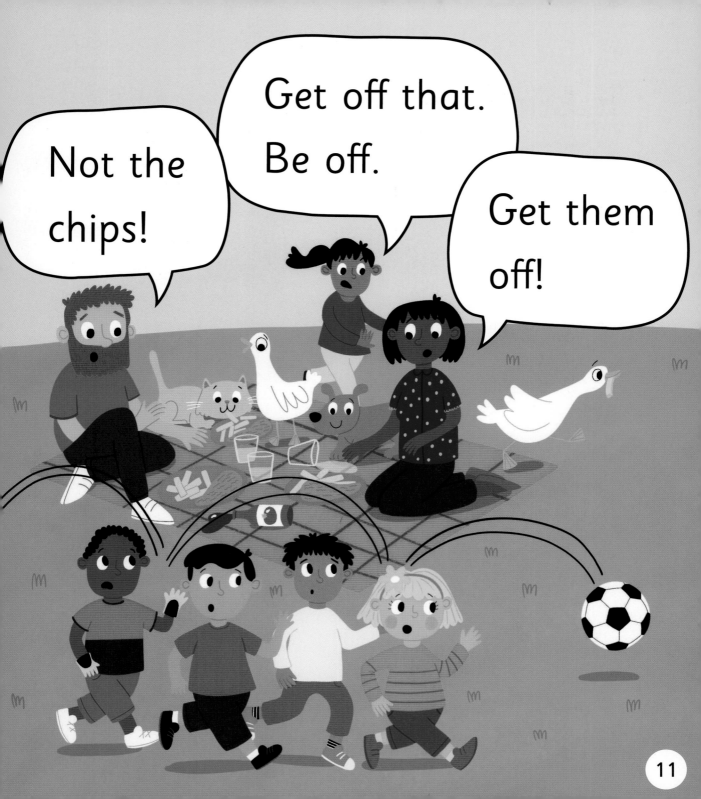

11

It is in with the chicks.

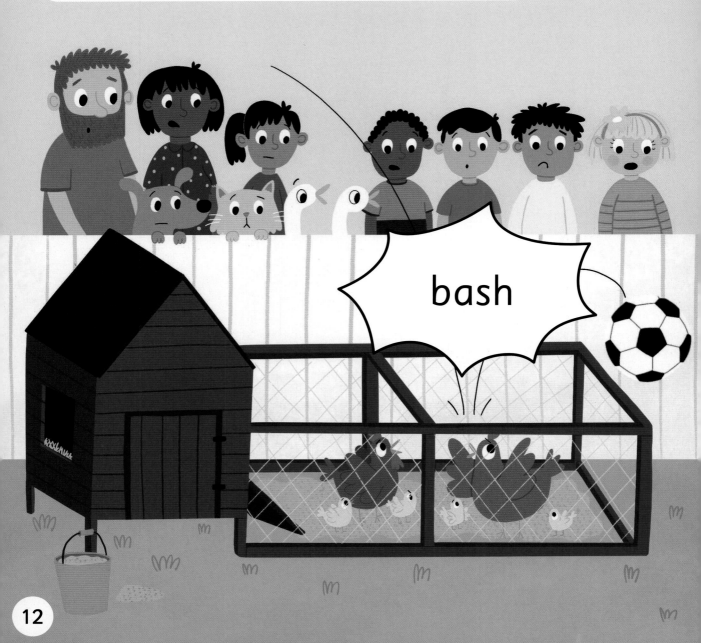

It hit the shop.

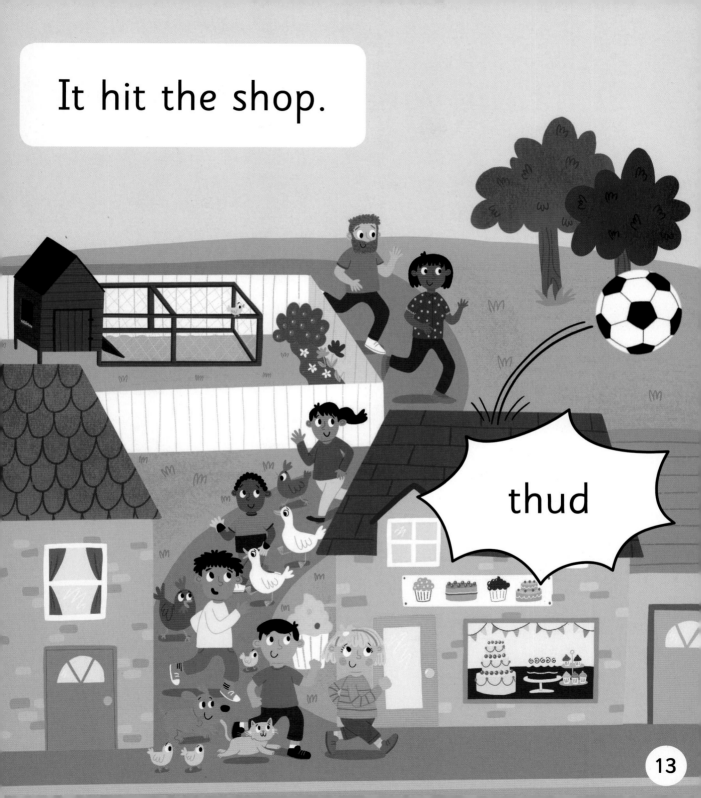

thud

13

It hit the van.

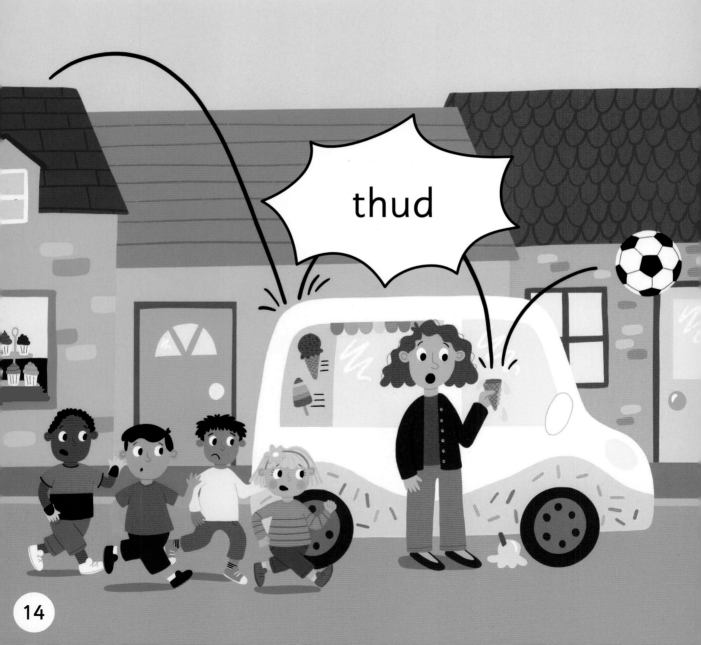

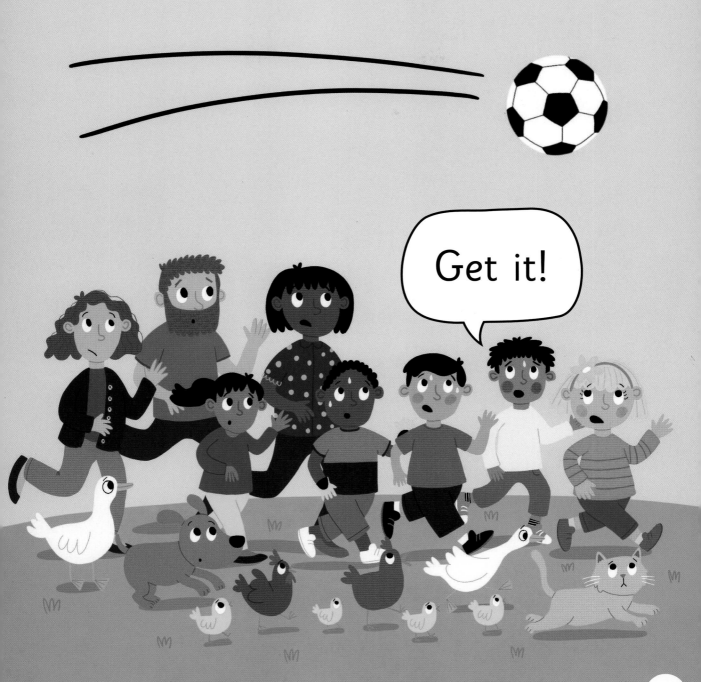

Shot! It is in.

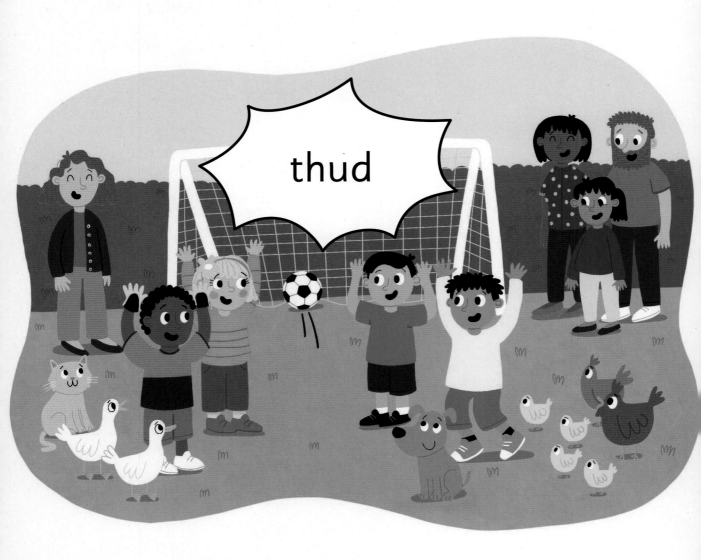